LAMDA
CONTEMPORARY MONOLOGUES FOR YOUNG MEN AND WOMEN
VOLUME II

Catherine Weate

Catherine has been voice coaching for over 20 years in England, Australia, Hong Kong and India. Her work has taken her into the diverse worlds of education, commerce, law, politics, theatre, film, television and radio. She has been Head of Voice at Rose Bruford College, Head of Voice and Vice Principal at the Academy of Live and Recorded Arts and Head of Examinations at LAMDA.

LAMDA
CONTEMPORARY MONOLOGUES FOR YOUNG MEN AND WOMEN
VOLUME II

Edited by Catherine Weate

PUBLISHED BY
OBERON BOOKS
FOR THE LONDON ACADEMY OF
MUSIC AND DRAMATIC ART

First published in this collection in 2007 for LAMDA Ltd.
by Oberon Books Ltd.
521 Caledonian Road, London N7 9RH
Tel: 020 7607 3637 / Fax: 020 7607 3629
e-mail: info@oberonbooks.com
www.oberonbooks.com

A catalogue record for this book is available from the British Library.

ISBN 1 84002 756 8 / 978-1-84002-756-3

Cover design: Joe Ewart for Society

Printed in Great Britain by Antony Rowe Ltd, Chippenham.

Contents

PART TWO: TWENTIES

Female

Male

PART THREE: THIRTIES

Female

Male

Introduction

Scouring plays to find a contemporary monologue for an audition or examination can be a time-consuming and elusive process. Everybody seems to be searching for something unique, attention-grabbing and personally challenging; in other words, a monologue from a new piece of writing with a fully-rounded character, who presents an interesting, and perhaps moving, self-contained story-line, which will help the performer to explore personal skills and capabilities. Not only are there vast numbers of newly published and performed works to read but there are specific factors that need to be taken into consideration, such as the character's age and cultural background, before emotional range and story can even be considered. A difficult task indeed.

Contemporary Monologues for Young Men and Women: Volume II provides the young performer with a wide range of contemporary material, organised into age-specific groups for ease of reference. All of the monologues have been chosen from plays published since 1985 and present characters from different countries and cultural backgrounds. Each piece is accompanied by a brief outline of the context and setting to assist the performer in staging and developing the character.

There are some fascinating stories to explore, from the historical (Polly Teale's fictionalised account of the three Brontë sisters in *Brontë*, or the modern day version of the Oresteia with Orestes and Electra as murderous teens in *The Murders at Argos* by David Foley) to the contemporary and controversial (Chris O'Connell's *Car*, which opens with the violent theft of a car by four boys, or the true story of Zahid Mubarek, who was murdered by his cellmate in Feltham Young Offenders Institution, in *Gladiator Games* by Tanika Gupta). I haven't shied away from including such controversial material, primarily because these plays are so incredibly well written but also because that is, essentially, the nature of much contemporary drama for young people.

Good luck with your search and I hope you find what you're looking for.

Catherine Weate

PART ONE: TEENS – FEMALE

THE MURDERS AT ARGOS
by David Foley

Originally commissioned by the Hyperion Theatre in Seattle, *The Murders at Argos* was first performed at the New York International Fringe Festival in August 2000.

The Murders at Argos *is a modern day (American) version of the Oresteia with Orestes and Electra as murderous teens. CHRYSOTHEMIS is their sister and, in this scene, she is talking to Orestes who has returned to Argos in order to avenge the death of their father by killing their mother and her lover. CHRYSOTHEMIS assumes (naively) that everything is going to be alright. Strong language is used throughout the play.*

CHRYSOTHEMIS: I'm so glad you're back!

She sits next to him and starts to roll the ball of yarn.

Now we're all together again. Except for Daddy. And Iphigeneia…

I was afraid. I can tell you now. Mommy didn't want you to come back. Electra said it was because you'd kill her if you did. But you wouldn't kill Mommy, would you? I can see that now. Electra always sees the worst in things. She's always so *dire*! But look! Here you are, and everything's fine. Oh, it's like a nightmare has passed! You know that feeling when you're running and running and you don't know what you're running from, but whatever it is is terrifying. And you want to scream, you want to scream for help, but you try and try and try and you can't. And if you can't scream, something horrible is going to happen. And then you wake up! And it was just a nightmare. And everything's fine. That's how I feel. Because we're all together now. I don't think I'm a cock-eyed optimist. I'm not an idiot – whatever Electra thinks. I know that terrible things have happened. I'm not blind. But the important thing is that we can be together now. We can get *beyond* it. Because when it comes right down to it, what do we have but each other? Really? And if we can – I don't mean to sound corny or sappy – but if we can just *love* each other – then maybe everything will be *all right!*

ORESTES rises with a cry and flings the yarn on the floor.

Orestes? What is it? Is something wrong?

She goes to him, but he strikes her away so that she falls to the floor.

[ORESTES: Leave me alone!]

CHRYSOTHEMIS: What? What did I say? Don't hit me! Don't hurt me!

Available in *The Murders at Argos / Cressida Among the Greeks*, published by Oberon Books Ltd. Reprinted by kind permission of the publisher.

ISBN: 1 84002 323 6 / 978 1 84002 323 7

THE MURDERS AT ARGOS

by David Foley

Originally commissioned by the Hyperion Theatre in Seattle, *The Murders at Argos* was first performed at the New York International Fringe Festival in August 2000.

David Foley, an American playwright, has updated the Oresteia for modern day audiences. Orestes has killed his mother and her lover to avenge the death of his father and is now on trial. His sister ELECTRA supports him and, in this scene, speaks to Tyndareus, her grandfather, in front of everybody, about who is really to blame for the tragedy. Strong language is used throughout the play.

ELECTRA: (*To TYNDAREUS.*) *Where is your shame?* Any of you? How dare you stand here and pretend to judge him? You talk of law and justice as if you knew what those words meant. Where is your shame!

If you kill my brother it won't be because of his alleged crime. It will be because he is an inconvenience to you. He is a sign of *your* disease and *your* corruption, and you'd just as soon not have to look at him.

Where was your justice when my father was murdered? Where were your noble ideals then? They weren't convenient. My mother was powerful so you laid aside your scruples and pretended nothing had happened. But now my brother comes and rights a terrible wrong, and you fall on him like birds of prey. Justice indeed!

How I admired you once. The brave men of Greece, sailing off to war. So strong. So glorious. I *believed* in you!

And now you've come back – the world laid waste because of you – and you dare to judge *us?*

You have failed us, your evil generation. You have bred us up in violence. You have made a religion of it. Then when *we* are violent, you turn on us. You tell us we're diseased and unnatural. Well, if we're diseased, who were the carriers? Who infected us?

If Orestes is guilty, then so are you. Condemn Orestes and you condemn yourselves. Remember, we are your children.

Her voice breaking a little.

We are your children.

A last childish whisper.

We are your children.

Available in *The Murders at Argos / Cressida Among the Greeks*, published by Oberon Books Ltd. Reprinted by kind permission of the publisher.

ISBN: 1 84002 323 6 / 978 1 84002 323 7

LOOK AT ME

by Anna Reynolds

Produced by the Mercury Theatre in association with Theatre Centre, *Look At Me* was first performed at the Mercury Studio, Colchester in October 1999.

The play intertwines the stories of two teenage girls facing exclusion from mainstream education. In this scene STACEY explains to John, one of her teachers and her mother's boyfriend, how she has locked another teacher in a cupboard. John asks her to prove everybody wrong and let her out. The final part of the speech is delivered directly to the audience.

STACEY: Mrs G asks me to get the video out of the video cupboard, right?

But the lead gets caught on something, I can't see what, and I'm pulling away at it, right, and she's shouting down the corridor, what's taking so long Stacey? and I'm getting really flustered because she thinks I'm stupid, she's always getting at me for not doing things right, being slow and that. So she comes down the corridor after me, I can hear those squeaky shoes getting nearer, and she's behind me –

– so I say, the lead's caught, miss, it's not my fault, I'm trying, and she pushes me out of the way/ and –

– and then she gives it a tug and the leads flies out. So simple. And she says, *can't you get anything right?* And then somehow I'm closing the door on her and before I know it I'm standing outside the cupboard, with the keys swinging from my hand.

I don't think she's frightened of anything, Sir. Anyhow
she's probably clawed her way out by now. You hate her as
much as I do. Let her sweat.

STACEY freezes JOHN.

Alright. What d'you think he's playin at? He don't care
about Mrs G any more than I do but… God, if only she
could stay in there for a little bit longer. Like a week?
He's sayin, let her out now and you're safe. Or he unlocks
her and she comes out of there like a bull and it's over,
I'm out, bye bye Stacey, have a nice life on the rubbish
heap. Just cause I don't wanna do this simple thing. (*She
pauses, like she's listening to someone.*) You think I should
let her out? I CAN'T HEAR YOU. Let her out? No. But,
'Surprise me', he says. 'Prove me wrong.' I hate it when
they say that.

Available in *Theatre Centre Plays for Young People Volume 1*,
published by Aurora Metro Press. Reprinted by kind permission of
the publisher.

ISBN: 0 9542330 5 0 / 978 0 9542330 5 1

GORGEOUS

by Anna Furse

Gorgeous was first performed in October 1999 at Mount Carmel School, London N19.

ALICE is a 15 year old girl living in Victorian England, who is magically transported through time to the present day where she confronts her own body image and an eating disorder. In this scene she has just experienced a fall, not unlike Alice in Wonderland, and finds herself in the 20th Century with some very strange objects, including a magazine with a picture of Leonardo Di Caprio, and she speaks her inner thoughts aloud. Another one of the objects is a mobile phone and when she accidentally gets through to the voicemail she hears the voice of a modern day version of herself and responds in confusion.

ALICE: "Leonardo – true love, the true story" (*She picks up a pair of Calvin Klein women's boxer short knickers. Admires them.*) I think Mother might approve of these. Well, they're grey. Cotton. Unadorned. Except perhaps they're a bit short... Maybe they belong to someone very small. (*Reads.*) "C.A.L.V.I.N. K.L.E.I.N" Hmm. That doesn't sound like a girl. (*Drops them.*) Ooooh! Maybe they're not girls'. Oh! What if they're boys'. (*Picks them up very fearfully and reads the label again.*) "One size. Washing instructions: machine wash forty and tumble dry?" Machine???? Tumble??? Why would Calvin want anyone to know these things about herself, or himself? (*She picks up a pair of platform shoes.*) Oooooh. I've seen pictures of these in my book about Greek Drama. (*Picks up a Wonderbra.*) What on earth could this be? (*Finds label and reads.*) *"Wonderbra"* what a strange word. "Thirty-four B cup"... must be some cooking thing. For measuring ingredients? Maybe for cheese-making? You could put the curds in here and hang it over... Certainly couldn't drink out of it. Feels nice. Reminds me of something but I cannot think what. (*Finds a make-up purse.*) Ah! I know what this is. Well, at least I think I do – no, maybe not... (*She opens lipsticks, blushers, eyeliners, mascaras and reads all the names and descriptions, puzzled and very interested e.g.*) "Titian Red", "Charcoal", "Irridescent Rose Madder"... Maybe it's some artist's bag. Wait a minute. (*Opens a powder compact.*) I think I know what this might be (*She sniffs it, dabs her finger on it, crumbles it in her fingers.*) Yes! I knew it! Powder paint!! Maybe Calvin is an artist. Maybe Leonardo is Leonardo Da Vinci and Calvin is his pupil... Maybe Calvin helped mix the colours for the Mona Lisa! Maybe he fell in love with her! But why the knickers? (*Finds a mobile phone.*) Gracious! What extraordinary material. Sort of like coal. No. Iron. No. I've never felt anything quite like it. Oh! It's got numbers on it! (*She explores the keys, accidentally punches a stored number and gets through.*)

[FUTURE ALICE: Hello. This is Alice's mobile voicemail. Please leave a message after you hear the beep, saying who you are and when you called and I'll get back to you when I can. Bye.]

ALICE: (*Amazed.*) It, it can't be – it sounds so familiar.

ALICE slams the phone down. Then cautiously picks it up and tries again. This time, after the voicemail message comes on again:

[FUTURE ALICE: Hello. This is Alice's mobile voicemail. Please leave a message after you hear the beep, saying who you are and when you called and I'll get back to you when I can. Bye.]

ALICE: Who are you? Are you in there? Can you hear me?! I'm Alice. I'm Alice Goodbody. And I'm very confused. I'm fifteen years old. Well, just. Today is actually my birthday. I'm just getting ready for my tea-party to celebrate. I have just turned fifteen. Just now. About to – I have just had the most extraordinary sensation of falling. Everything looks the same, only different somehow.

Available in *Theatre Centre Plays for Young People Volume 1*, published by Aurora Metro Press. Reprinted by kind permission of the publisher.

ISBN: 0 9542330 5 0 / 978 0 9542330 5 1

BURN

by Deborah Gearing

Burn was originally part of the NT Shell Connections 2005 programme, and was first performed in July 2005 by Wired Youth Theatre. It received its first professional production in March 2006 at the National Theatre in London.

Birdman is 15 years old and without family and friends. Burn *is the story of his last day. The teenagers that knew him are down by the riverbank and relate the events that led to his death. Here, RACHEL, who is 16, picks up the story. She speaks to her friends.*

RACHEL: It was after eight when I saw Birdman.
    How I know –
    it's a bit complicated – I'll start at the beginning.
    Me sitting listening for Col –
    he's always late –
    sitting listening to that little gold clock on the mantelshelf.
    It chimes on the half-hour – just once
    then on the full hour it does the whole works –
    me sitting listening to it chime eight times –
    he's late he's late he's late he's late.
    Me sitting listening on the edge of my seat –
    I can't sit back because I'll put creases in my top.
    At eight he's late.
    Well late.

    I'm beginning to think he's gone off with someone else
    Mel or Linda or Jackie or Marie – they'd all go with him –
    he's only got to whistle.
    That's a line from a film, but he meant it nice.
    I mean – they're dogs – and they're nothing to him.

I'm beginning to think I'll chuck that little gold clock out
the window
I'm beginning to think I'm not feeling too good – I'm
beginning to shrink on the inside, and my mouth's all dry.
Then the doorbell rings.

Doorbell.

That's him.
And in a minute we're gonna go out
and in a minute we're gonna kiss
and in a minute we're gonna get all loved-up.

Hang on a minute Col. I just need to get my shoes.
Where's my handbag? Okay.

Available in *Burn / Rosalind*, published by Oberon Books Ltd.
Reprinted by kind permission of the publisher.

ISBN: 1 84002 659 6 / 978 1 84002 659 7

BLUE

by Ursula Rani Sarma

Blue was commissioned by the Cork Opera House in 2000 and was first performed in the Half Moon Theatre in June 2000.

DANNY (Daniella) is a tomboy in her late teens but looks younger than her age. She lives in an isolated sea-side town in Ireland and her best friends are Joe and Des. DANNY is an epileptic and is bullied by the other girls in her class. Here, she describes one of her fits to the audience after being chased by some of the bullies. Strong language is used throughout the play.

DANNY: I lean against the wall for a while
    and then I turn for home,
    but they're still behind me,
    they're throwing gravel at the back of my legs.
    My head is still swimming.
    Try to get away, have to get away

More laughter.

Debbie Wilson…I swear I…

Breaks.

I…please…
please…
I don't feel so good

More laughter.

and my head is spinning and I'm screaming at them.
Something flips into place and I'm
tearing down towards the strand,
have to find the lads,

Joe Leary will sort you out you fat cow,
Or Des…
Des…

They're all on the strand,
the lads are playing football or skimming stones but
I'm looking for the lads,
can't see Des.
Mrs Combers comes over and wants to know why won't
I play with the rest of them,
I try and explain,
there's a roaring in my ears and I can't hear myself talk,

Lighting change to isolate her, she physically reacts as if a needle has been stuck between her eyes, in obvious pain for the rest of this speech, it is slow and drugged.

am I talking at all?
She's looming over me,
she's like a great beached whale, I think,
and then I tell her,
you're like a great-beached whale Mrs Combers, did you
know that?
But the banging gets louder and louder,
and my leg starts to shake,
I'm looking at it,

Falls to her knees, rocking forward and back.

but I can't stop it,
and then the other one starts,
Mrs Combers face is getting redder and redder,
looks like it's going to explode,
I try to tell her but

Lights cut to a single strobe, she moves in the light for a moment, rocking back onto her heels and then coming up to kneel facing the audience, calmer now.

it's like someone reaches in to my head and changes the frequency, with a warm liquid hand, and all I can feel is a sweet heat spreading up from my tummy, and a smile to match on my face, and then everything is perfect, and it all goes dark.

Available in *...touched... / Blue*, published by Oberon Books Ltd. Reprinted by kind permission of the publisher.

ISBN: 1 84002 269 8 / 978 1 84002 269 8

PLAYING FROM THE HEART

by Charles Way

Playing from the Heart was commissioned by Polka Theatre for Children, Wimbledon, London, where it was first performed in 1998.

Playing from the Heart *explores the early life of EVELYN GLENNIE, who became a renowned percussionist despite her profound deafness. In this scene, EVELYN is playing in a school ensemble at the Royal Albert Hall and speaks her inner thoughts aloud.*

EVELYN: I can hear you thinking –
   I can hear you thinking –
   What's going on?
   What on earth is she about to do –
   This girl in a party dress?
   This is it, you see.
   The moment.
   All my life I've worked
   for this moment.
   They say I will never be a musician
   today I will prove them wrong.
   This is it.
   The orchestra's ready.
   The audience applaud
   as the conductor walks
   in his black suit across the stage.
   I feel his steps
   in the wood beneath my feet.
   I feel the sound of clapping
   in the tense air of the concert hall.
   I watch the faces of the people,
   the movement of their hands.

Of course it could all go wrong.
I could lose my way
In the great forest of notes.
No! I must concentrate.
I must succeed.
I will succeed.
I am me –
Me is a very determined person.
This is it – the moment.
The conductor raises his baton,
The audience breathe in –

An intake of air.

– the baton hovers in the air
Holding time
Holding time.
A bead of sweat runs down
the conductor's cheek.
How slowly it falls…
How slowly…

Sound of heart beat.

But wait!
What's happening?
What sound is that?
The sound of my heart
slowing down…
slowing down…

Available in *Plays for Young People* by Charles Way, published by
Aurora Metro Press. Reprinted by kind permission of the publisher.

ISBN: 0 9536757 1 8 / 978 0 9536757 1 5

ROSALIND

by Deborah Gearing

Rosalind: A Question of Life was first presented by Birmingham Repertory Theatre on a schools tour in September 2005. The first public performance by Birmingham Repertory Theatre was at The Door in November 2005.

Rosalind: A Question of Life *tells the story of Rosalind Franklin who helped discover the structure of DNA, only to be written out of the history books. ESTHER is in her late teens and is studying to be a scientist. She is convinced that biochemistry is the way forward but her brother, Joe, isn't sure and raises some moral dilemmas. Then Rosalind appears and they find themselves re-enacting her life and entering into the debate. In this scene, Joe and ESTHER are remembering the time ESTHER lost a science quiz when she was 14 years old.*

ESTHER: I flunked it, Joe. But not because of that boy. I lost my concentration. I was too tired or something. Somebody coughed. And it was you, Joe.

You coughing. And then I looked. And you looked just like dad – and I felt this terrible – whoosh – I missed dad. It went right through me.

It's funny how things flash through your mind sometimes – how quickly you can think – like three films at once, all playing at once. I thought so many things in thirty seconds – I remembered when I said I wanted to be a scientist at tea one day. And they laughed and said – you could be a doctor. That'd be good, a doctor in the family. And I said – no – I want to be a research scientist – work in a lab, do experiments. And dad said – it will be useful, won't it? Is that useful? And you sat there in the audience, coughing just like dad, and I couldn't believe he'd gone. It was like he was in the room. And then I remembered coming home from school, and gran was sitting there crying. And I'd never seen her cry before. And it was all creepy quiet. No radio. She always had the radio on. Crying for her boy. My dad. He'd had a massive asthma attack and his heart had given way. His poor heart. And then you came home and she had to tell it all over again. And it didn't change, the way she told it – it was like – she couldn't find any other words to say it. There just aren't any other words.

My boy, she said. My boy.

And so – when I heard you coughing I just suddenly missed dad. And it was quiet around me, I was far away. And I didn't care about winning. I just really didn't care. I just wanted dad back.

Available in *Burn / Rosalind*, published by Oberon Books Ltd. Reprinted by kind permission of the publisher.

ISBN: 1 84002 659 6 / 978 1 84002 659 7

STAMPING, SHOUTING AND SINGING HOME

by Lisa Evans

Stamping, Shouting and Singing Home was commissioned and first performed by Watford Palace Theatre-in-Education Company in 1986.

The play is set in 1950s America and Lizzie and her family are still experiencing the everyday injustices reserved for black Americans in the Deep South. However, the world is on the brink of change and Lizzie's older sister MARGUERITE decides to fight back. In this speech, she describes for her mother and Lizzie what happens when she tries to eat in a café usually reserved for white people.

MARGUERITE: I didn't plan on staying out late Mama. It was light when I went in. It was real crowded but only a few folks sitting outside at them pretty tables on the sidewalk. So I went and sat there too. Folks were staring like I come from Mars or someplace. You think my skin green not brown. But I didn't take notice. I sat at the table and waited for the waitress. Pretty soon she come out and took an order from the table next to mine. Then she goes back inside. Through the glass I could see white folks nudging and laughing at me, and the waitress talking to the manager. She come out with the order for the next table. This time I say, 'Excuse me Miss.' But she act like I wasn't there. No voice. No sound. But I heard my voice. And I heard it again when next she pass and I say, very polite, 'I'd like a cup of coffee, please.' I ask three more times but she carries on acting like I'm invisible. Then it come on to rain. But I sat on. I sat on while it got dark and they turned up the lights inside. And folks came and went and had coffee and cake and talked and laughed together. And I sat on. Pretending I didn't care. They weren't going to drive me away. Flood could have come and I'd have stayed, sitting in the dark, rain on the window panes, running down my back till I didn't rightly know if I was turned to stone. Some cars hooted as they drove off, laughing and yelling foul words. But I sat on. I had a right to be sitting there. I had a right to be served coffee just like they did. So I sat on. Then they closed up, put out the lights. I got up and come home.

Available in *Stamping, Shouting and Singing Home*, published by Oberon Books Ltd. Reprinted by kind permission of the publisher.

ISBN: 1 84002 703 7 / 978 1 84002 703 7

PART ONE: TEENS – MALE

WISE GUYS

by Philip Osment

Wise Guys was first performed in October 1997 by Theatre Centre and Red Ladder Theatre Company.

MIKE is caught up in a self-destructive cycle, with an abusive bully for a father and a life of petty crime. Will he be able to change and break free of the cycle? In this scene, at the beginning of the play, MIKE speaks to the audience about his life. Strong language is used throughout the play.

MIKE: My brother Martin looks like one of those kids you
    see on TV at Christmas singing carols. Angelic. He's not.
    But he looks like it. I always felt like I had to protect him.
    'Cos he was so much younger. I've been mean to him,
    don't get me wrong. Stole my Walkman and broke it one
    time. Closest I ever came to losing it with him. I mean
    I thumped him but not like to really hurt him. I'd never
    do that. At the end of the day he's the only person I care
    about. And I'm the only person he cares about. My Mum
    says I got too much influence over him. She's scared I'm
    going to lead him astray. I nearly got done for nicking
    car stereos and she's scared I'll get him into that. But I
    wouldn't. I'd kill him if he started that.

There's three of us usually.

Skid smashes the window, I take the stereo out and Darren
stands by with a rucksack and a bike to take it home.
Like that. Very easy. Very safe. At the end of the day you
don't get a lot each but there ain't much chance of getting
caught. The person taking the stereo home has got the
worst job 'cos mine takes two seconds, his takes, what?
Ten minutes max.

Skid reckons I'm criminally minded. I walk down a street and I notice things that someone who weren't criminally minded wouldn't notice.

It's not nice. It's not normal. Like I see a laptop on a car seat or someone's wallet hanging out their back pocket. Or a door to a house left open. I notice them things.

Available in *Plays for Young People* by Philip Osment, published by Oberon Books Ltd. Reprinted by kind permission of the publisher.

ISBN: 1 84002 272 8 / 978 1 84002 272 8

MANCUB

by Douglas Maxwell

(Adapted from the book
The Flight of the Cassowary by John LeVert)

Mancub was commissioned by Vanishing Point and opened at the Traverse Theatre, Edinburgh in May 2005.

PAUL is a Scottish teenager facing all the usual struggles of growing up. As his stresses increase, he retreats into the world of the animal kingdom. In this scene, PAUL talks to the audience about his struggle to approach girls and, for the first time, notices that people around him display the traits of certain animals.

PAUL: Walking home about 19 yards behind Karen. Watching every step. Every wiggle. Imagining the fabric around her body. Trying to remember her smell. Get it? Got it.

How do folk ask folk out? It's a mystery.

I can't speak to her face to face. That's insanity.

I can't phone her. That'd be worse. We've got one phone and it's in the kitchen. Everyone listens. If you're on for more than twenty-five seconds the King Of The Ants starts hopping in front of you pointing at his watch and miming money.

I can just imagine her

– guess which little fanny phoned up my house last night? I was like, no way man.

But it must happen somehow. People have girlfriends. Some people even have sex. They must do, I've seen it on TV.

She's surrounded by guys as always.

It reminds me of birds.

Male birds can only attract a female by showing off. Same as us. This school is an adolescent aviary.

The girls watch as we bump bellies and hop.

We have our crowing cockerels, our singing thrushes, our mocking mocking birds, a whole flock of us stomping the ground as the girls chew gum and send text messages.

I don't want any of that. I want to be an eagle. They don't dance or fight to get attention. They just circle, higher and higher, until they're a speck. Then they fold and plummet to the ground. Eyes wide open.

Faster faster faster faster

Closer closer closer closer

And just before they smash into the ground...wings... land...silent.

That would impress her. If I was an eagle.

Available in *Mancub*, published by Oberon Books Ltd. Reprinted by kind permission of the publisher.

ISBN: 1 84002 475 5 / 978 1 84002 475 3

TREEHOUSES

by Elizabeth Kuti

Treehouses was first performed at the Peacock Theatre, Dublin in April 2000.

A Jewish BOY, 15 or 16 years of age, escapes deportation and possible death during World War II by hiding in the local farmer's barn. The farmer's daughter, Magda, takes care of him and here he talks to her for the first time about what has happened to him.

BOY: I kept telling them we had to leave, I kept telling them – I've known for ages we had to go – all of us, we just should have gone, I kept telling them, but they wouldn't, they said we couldn't – but we knew, everyone knew. Every night central station was packed with people – we all knew about it – and trains going every night at three, four in the morning, trains going when there shouldn't have been any trains. I saw them ages ago, I walked past once at three in the morning, I was coming home from work in the restaurant, and I saw all these hundreds of people being jammed onto trains. And I looked up and all around the station in apartment blocks there were people looking out of windows, watching – and they all saw this going on – they saw, they knew – And everyone was talking about resettlement then, about persons being resettled in other provinces – but it didn't look right to me, I knew at the time it wasn't right – their faces were – the faces of the people – I don't know – it looked wrong to me. So I stopped and asked this guard – it was dark, he couldn't see my face so I asked him what was going on – where the trains were going – was this a resettlement programme, and what province were these people going to? And he laughed and said don't worry son, these trains are going east and all these people have got a one-way ticket, and I said what do you mean going east, to what province. And he laughed again and said, to another sort of province altogether.

And I told my father this and I said I thought we should go then, we should have gone then, we should have walked out with nothing in our hands, we just should just have gone, we should have, we should have, we should have just walked –

Available in *Treehouses*, published by A & C Black Publishers. Reprinted by kind permission of the publisher.

ISBN: 0 413 75380 8 / 978 0 413 75380 9

BURN

by Deborah Gearing

Burn was originally part of the NT Shell Connections 2005 programme and was first performed in July 2005 by Wired Youth Theatre. It received its first professional production in March 2006 at the National Theatre in London.

Burn *is about a 15 year old loner, Birdman, and the events that led to his death. The teenagers that knew him are down by the riverbank and tell the story of his last day. AARON is 15 as well and was the first person who saw Birdman that day. He speaks to his friends.*

AARON: Early in the morning.
    Birdman came to see me.
    It was early in the morning
    on that particular day.

The red glow fades to daylight.

Riverbank.

AARON, Sal loaded down with fishing rods and a plastic bag, Birdman.

Hear this.
Sea tang rising off the river.
I'm out of bed and down the stairs.
Birdman's waiting.
With his board.
Not boards, I say. Not today.
Smell that –
Birdman flaring his nostrils in the wind
like some beast.
Wolf.

Me and Sal, we're the pack.
But today I'm leading.
It's my shout.
(How Sal come to be part of this I don't want to tell –
tag-along, tell-tale, carry-all or I'll kick you down the
bank.)
Come on, I say. Come on.
And we leave the Manor
heading for that white bridge that swoops
across the river.
Hogweed, cow parsley, rush, sedge, madder.
(Yeah, it's a girl thing, plants,
But I like the way they sound.)
I've got my stick
and a steady rhythm –
thwack, step, thwack, step, thwack.
Heads flying. Backs broken.
Smells – rank.
But we've got a steady pace –
I don't let up – sun's moving up
over the river.
Flies buzzing.
It's two miles down the river.
We're keeping step. Then.
Full stop.
Fence.
Railway line.
Sal
(sniveller, snot-maker, here blow it or I'll burn you to a
cinder).
Birdman. Me.

Available in *Burn / Rosalind*, published by Oberon Books.
Reprinted by kind permission of the publisher.

ISBN: 1 84002 659 6 / 978 1 84002 659 7

BLUE

by Ursula Rani Sarma

Blue was commissioned by the Cork Opera House in 2000 and was first performed in the Half Moon Theatre in June 2000.

JOE lives in an isolated sea-side town in Ireland and only has a week to go before he finishes school. He and his friends Des and Danny (short for Daniella) have a ritual of jumping into the sea from the cliff tops and for a few seconds on the way down they feel alive and believe that anything is possible. In this scene, JOE expresses his frustration of living in a small town to the audience, just before another jump. Strong language is used throughout the play.

JOE: 'The rest of the world could set itself by the way the day goes in this shagging place', by Joe Leary.

Clears his throat.

Look at us, we live just like the hands of a clock, every day we do the same things, wake up, go to school, go to swim practice, get yelled at by my Da, up here to the point straight after, listen to Danny moan about jumping off, jump off, go home, eat dinner, pretend to study, go to bed. Friday nights we go into town, Saturdays we watch videos in Danny's house and Sundays we play PlayStation in my house. And it's just…well it's so boring, but there isn't anything else to do, we're probably the most active people in the whole shagging town, everyone does the same thing minute by minute, hour by hour…that's why you could set a clock by this place.

We didn't think it was so bad to be doing the same things for the past seventeen years 'cos we didn't know any better. We've been isolated from the rest of the universe, it's like a bloody third world down here.

We might as well be in feckin Calcutta, you know my cousin Dave in Dublin? He had a choice of twenty-three subjects for the leaving last year and they went to Croatia on their school tour, we have to do the eight we're told to do and we go to Bunratty Castle on our tours. The cinemas and the clubs and everything…they have loads of things to do.

And what do we have…we have the Atlantic…and fair enough, they don't have the Atlantic, but for me, for a chance to get a slice of the bigger something, I'd trade her for that bit of excitement any day, any day.

Right so.

Stands and turns to an imaginary string of cattle and begins.

Ladies and gentlemen, observe if you will the double twist with the one half backward tumble performed by none other than our very own, Daniella Buckley.

Available in *…touched… / Blue*, published by Oberon Books Ltd. Reprinted by kind permission of the publisher.

ISBN: 1 84002 269 8 / 978 1 84002 269 8

BLUE

by Ursula Rani Sarma

Blue was commissioned by the Cork Opera House in 2000 and was first performed in the Half Moon Theatre in June 2000.

DES is in his late teens and lives in an isolated seaside town in Ireland. It is his very last day of school and important swimming heats are to take place the following day. If he wins a medal he has a chance of securing a scholarship to Berkley so he decides to skip a soccer match to train. Here he explains to the audience how he is caught by one of the teachers. Strong language is used throughout the play.

DES: Outside the day is so beautiful I want to cry,
    the road is hot already,
    sticking tar to the soles of my shoes,
    I turn out from our gate and see her there before me,
    all shimmering and shining in her milky blues and greens,
    We have grey summers here,
    but not today, look at it,
    they won't do a tap in the school
    last day today and they'll only be giving awards for the best footballer and the best hurler,
    the exams though,
    I get a burning in my chest when I think about them,
    but it's the last day though,
    and the heats are tomorrow.

    I go straight for the pool,
    I can see the lads are all only down the strand anyway.
    Playing soccer,
    I want to train,
    I strip to my shorts and there's no one there but me.

The water's like a sheet,
I dive through and start to stroke.
Find the rhythm.
Two hundred percent in the water, two hundred percent
concentration.
Cut through the water like a knife.
Feel my body change gears like an engine and this is it,
I feel it.
This is the first day of something else.

I'm well into it now,
must be on my twentieth lap or so,
when I see him standing at the side of the pool,
my lungs freeze,
he doesn't look happy.
I swim to the side and
'good morning sir,
No sir,
what?
Special, sir, no I don't think I'm special it's just with the
heats tomorrow I –
But I don't play soccer I –
And with three words he shatters everything that was
perfect about today,
Off the team
But I'm team captain sir –
It's tomorrow sir,
the medal, the scholarship,
You can't do that sir,

Available in *...touched...* / *Blue*, published by Oberon Books Ltd.
Reprinted by kind permission of the publisher.

ISBN: 1 84002 269 8 / 978 1 84002 269 8

LISTEN TO YOUR PARENTS
by Benjamin Zephaniah

Produced in collaboration with Nottingham Playhouse Roundabout TIE, *Listen To Your Parents* was first performed in September 2002 in Nottingham.

MARK is a teenager living in Birmingham. He is passionate about football and has been spotted by a talent scout from Aston Villa who wants him to attend the junior team trials. His other love is writing poetry, which helps him to express his feelings about football, the girl he fancies, living in poverty and his violent father. In this speech he talks to the audience about his life.

MARK: Wali is me best friend, but he just don't know what's really going on. Everything would be alright if I get in that squad guy, it would be like a dream come true. I can't lose this chance. You should of seen me in school today, I played some wicked football. I'm serious, I was right on form, you should have seen me, I scored four goals and I helped set up two, so I know I can do it. (*Beat.*) But I wish I could practise at home. The family downstairs got that big garden to themselves but they can't use it because of the neighbours. I would use it anyway – I don't care if they call me black, I'll call them white. A garden would be so cool guy. I hate this house. Mom said that one day we'll live in a whole house instead of a silly little flat and we'll have our own bathroom. Carlton won't have to sleep with Mom and Dad, and I won't have to sleep in the same room as a girl. I want a garden guy, to practise me skills. (*Beat.*) And guess what? Maria Shah said that I can go to her birthday party next week. She hasn't even invited Wali, only me. And I was told that most of the kids there will be girls, only a few special boys are going and I'm one of them. Well, she keeps asking me to read poems to her innit? 'Cause I mek her laugh all the time. She's always watching me when I'm playing football, now she wants me to go to her party, she likes me innit, yeah guy she wants me badly. She smells like baked beans but I still like her, but I ain't going to tell her that, am I? Anyway I think football's more important now. (*Beat.*) Me Mom, that's who I really love. I know hundreds of kids say that about their Moms and everyone thinks their Mom's special but my Mom is. She ain't perfect. No one's perfect, but she's tough and she sticks by me, innit?

Available in *Theatre Centre Plays for Young People Volume 1*, published by Aurora Metro Press. Reprinted by kind permission of the publisher.

ISBN: 0 9542330 5 0 / 978 0 9542330 5 1

PRIVATE PEACEFUL

by Michael Morpurgo, adapted by Simon Reade

Private Peaceful was first performed in April 2004 at Bristol Old Vic's Studio Theatre.

This play is based on Michael Morpurgo's moving tale about 17 year old TOMMO PEACEFUL, who spends his last night during World War I reliving the events that led him to this juncture in time. Here he remembers, for the audience, a tense moment in trench warfare.

TOMMO: Word has come down from headquarters that we must send out patrols to find out what regiments have come into the line opposite us. Why we have to do this we do not know – there are spotter planes doing it almost every day. My turn soon comes up. Charlie's too. Captain Wilkie's heading the patrol and he tells us 'we have to bring back a prisoner for questioning'. He gives us a double rum ration, and I'm warmed instantly to the roots of my hair, to my very toenails.

On the signal, we climb over the top and crawl on our bellies through the wire.

We snake our way forward. It takes an eternity to cross no-man's-land. I begin to wonder if we'll ever find their trenches at all. We slither into a shell hole and lie doggo there for a while. We can hear Fritz talking now, and laughing – and playing music.

Sound: a distant gramophone plays.

We're close now, very close. I'm not scared – I'm excited. I'm out poaching with Charlie. I'm tensed for danger.

Then we see the wire up ahead. We wriggle through a gap and drop down into their trench.

It looks deserted, but we can still hear the voices and the music. I notice the trench is much deeper than ours, wider too and more solidly constructed. I grip my rifle tight and follow Charlie along the trench, bent double like everyone else.

We're making too much noise. I can't understand why no one has heard us. Where are their sentries, for God's sake?

At that moment, a German soldier comes out of a dug-out. For a split-second the Hun does nothing and neither do we. We just stand and look at one another. Then he lets out a shriek, blunders back into the dug-out. I don't know who threw the grenade in after him, (*Sound: blast.*) but there is a blast that throws me back against the trench wall. There is screaming and firing from inside the dug-out. Then silence. The music has stopped.

Available in *Private Peaceful, Aladdin and the Enchanted Lamp, The Owl Who Was Afraid of the Dark*, published by Oberon Books Ltd. Reprinted by kind permission of the publisher.

ISBN: 1 84002 660 X / 978 1 84002 660 3

PART TWO: TWENTIES – FEMALE

CARRYING SHOES INTO THE UNKNOWN
by Rosemary Johns

Carrying Shoes into the Unknown was first produced at La Mama Theatre, Melbourne in August 2005.

This is a fictionalised account of a true story of a Western family living in Iran during the last days of the Shah and the rise of Ayatollah Khomeini in the late 1970s. We meet ALICE as the play opens and she arrives at the airport in Iran from Australia where she has been working as a nurse. Her (English) parents have been living in Iran for some time and are supposed to meet her plane but they haven't turned up. The monologue explores her uncertainty and fear about what to do next as all her cultural expectations are challenged. ALICE speaks her thoughts aloud.

ALICE: What is this place? Where are Mum and Dad? They should be here?

I'm sweating with fear. Stop panicking, Alice. Get a grip. Breathe. Look. Plastic. New. It's an airport. You are fine. They will turn up, they always do…

Breathe… All those thousands of people in black… some massive political demonstration on the runway. There must be an important person on the plane. No one's interested in you.

What about the American guy? Coming out of nowhere, grabbing me, in his arms, pushing through the crowds screaming, pushing, shoving. 'Honey, come to my hotel, this is no place for a girl.' 'My parents are here… somewhere.' 'Are you blind, sweetheart? There's not one Western face here.' 'I'll be fine. They'll be here.' 'You're crazy, sweetheart. You should never have left home. This is dangerous. I'd be outta this hell if it weren't for the money. They want to tear us to pieces like confetti.'

I should have gone with him. I lost my chance… What do I do? Do I wait? Do I get a taxi? They've never let me down. They will turn up. I know it.

Breathe. You were right to refuse his offer to stay at his hotel. Anything could have happened. Deep breaths. You are a grown woman you have completed two years of nurse's training.

And I'm the only Western woman in a totally dysfunctional airport.

There is no wolf under the bed. Five years old looking under every bed for the wolf. There is no wolf. Stop looking for the wolf. Say the rhyme about the baby shoe. Don't be stupid. But the baby shoe protects you. That's why it's cast in brass. Remember the rhyme. The rhyme to stop being scared.

'There was an old woman who lived in a shoe,
A wolf left her baby all battered and chewed,
So off she went to get baby a coffin,
But when she came back… baby was laughin'.'

Why did Dad teach me such a weird rhyme at five years old? Both my parents are seriously weird. I'll forgive you if you just turn up. I'll forgive you everything, for not letting me wear make-up, for vetting my boyfriends.

There are no phones. There's no electricity… *Just come!*

Mum always insists on arriving hours early. What's happened to them? Some car accident? Something bad.

Take charge. What would they say at Manly Hospital: 'Grit your teeth, Alice, and wash the bed pans'.

I am gritting my teeth… with a smile. I'm up shit creek!

Forget the suitcase, it ain't coming. The airport's broken down… *Outside!*

Taxis!

Excuse me, can you please take me – He *spat* at me.

Please can you… this address… Old Shimran Road. Do you speak English? No need to swear at me.

What would Sister Mackey do? 'You're not bleeding, you're not dead. You must be right as rain.'

Not for hire?

No? There's no one else here. Why won't you take me?

One of them's walking toward me.

Have all my money… if you take me.

Extract from *Carrying Shoes into the Unknown* © Rosemary Johns, 2006. Reproduced by permission from Currency Press Pty Ltd, Sydney Australia.

ISBN: 0 86819 787 4 / 978 0 86819 787 6

PRECIOUS BANE

Adapted by Bryony Lavery
from the novel by Mary Webb

The world premiere production of *Precious Bane* was by Pentabus Theatre, in association with English Heritage and the National Trust, at Walcot Hall in Shropshire in July 2003.

This play is based on Mary Webb's story about a young woman, PRUDENCE SARN, in rural early 19th century England. PRUE's brother Gideon intended to marry Jancis Beguildy but events overtook the couple and he withdrew his promise. Jancis turns up on the Sarn doorstep with a tiny baby boy of which Gideon is the father. Gideon refuses to recognise the baby and storms off. Here, PRUE describes for the audience what happens next.

PRUE: I came into the kitchen
    the settle was empty
    I ran across the fold
    and out through the gate into the road…
    I canna find Jancis!

    her mother's dead
    her father's in prison!
    there must be somewhere else to look…
    oh think of somewhere quick!
    if not….

    we went down to the mere
    there
    just where the causeway went into the water
    was one of the baby's boots
    they lay there in a bed of lily leaves
    and we took them up without a word
    and carried them within

I washed them
and dressed them in white
and laid them on Mother's bed
and I mounded it up with flowers

white lilac
and thorn
and golden day-lilies
and golden cowslip
that the child should have made
into tossy balls
in the time to come

Still Gideon said nothing.
the night afore we took them to the churchyard
I heard him
he was standing by the bed
he stretches his hand out
fingers the plait of golden hair
he touches the plait of golden hair
that was ever the pride of poor Jancis

Available in *Precious Bane*, published by Oberon Books Ltd.
Reprinted by kind permission of the publisher.

ISBN: 1 84002 386 4 / 978 1 84002 386 2

THE MURDERS AT ARGOS

by David Foley

Originally commissioned by the Hyperion Theatre in Seattle, *The Murders at Argos* was first performed at the New York International Fringe Festival in August 2000.

The Greek tragedy of the Oresteia has been updated by an American playwright for modern day audiences with Orestes and Electra as murderous teens. Their older sister IPHIGENEIA was sacrificed by their father, Agamemnon, in order to raise some wind to sail off to war with Troy. In this scene, IPHIGENEIA appears to Electra and it seems that she didn't die after all. Strong language is used throughout the play.

IPHIGENEIA: Electra?

It's me, Electra. It's Iphigeneia.

Don't you recognize me?

(*Matter-of-factly.*) No. No, I'm not dead.

I was sacrificed. On a fine sunny day with no breeze – no breeze at all – I was led up to the altar, sprinkled with barley, and my throat was slit with a fine, sharp iron knife.

Yes, this is where it gets confusing. Artemis – unwilling to have her altar stained with innocent blood – made a last-minute substitution – a deer, I think – and whisked me away to a distant barbarous country to serve as priestess in her temple. (*Showing her throat.*) You see? Not even a scar.

The gods can do anything – though they don't usually do you any favors. For more years than I care to count, I have lived in a wretched little temple by the side of a lake. My only company is the priest – some benighted boob who knows only that the prescribed rituals must be followed to the letter. And so whenever some poor schmuck happens to wander onto the grounds, he must die for his impiety. The priest sees to that. Something with a stone knife and lots of blood. Then it's my job as priestess to dispose of the corpse and mop up the blood. Such is the service of the gods. I sometimes suspect Artemis of arranging the whole drama because she was short a priestess in her temple.

Available in *The Murders at Argos / Cressida Among the Greeks*, published by Oberon Books Ltd. Reprinted by kind permission of the publisher.

ISBN: 1 84002 323 6 / 978 1 84002 323 7

CRESSIDA AMONG THE GREEKS
by David Foley

Cressida Among the Greeks was first performed at the Ohio Theatre in New York City in February 2002.

Cressida Among the Greeks *is an updated version of Shakespeare's 'Troilus and Cressida' and explores love and betrayal amidst the chaos of war. The god Apollo gave the gift of prophecy to CASSANDRA, Troilus' sister, but also made sure that her visions of the future would not be believed. CASSANDRA foretells the downfall of her family and the city of Troy, which is currently under siege from the Greeks but, of course, no one will listen to her. Here, she questions her own sanity whilst her family ignore her and discuss the progress of the war. Strong language is used throughout the play.* .

CASSANDRA: Am I mad?

> They say if someone's mad, they never think themselves mad. They cannot ask, 'Am I mad?' Therefore, since I *have* asked, 'Am I mad?' then *ipso facto* I must not be mad.
>
> But this is subtle. Since I've just proved that I'm *not* mad, I therefore don't believe I'm mad. And for that very reason I may very well be mad.
>
> And why shouldn't I be mad? I've seen enough. You'd go crazy, too, if everywhere you looked – east, west, north, south – you saw the future bearing down upon you.
>
> Now Calchas isn't mad. No one saner. (*Contemptuously.*) 'Professional prophet.' Spills a few entrails, throws some sticks, consults the 'oracle'. Reading the signs. 'Oh, an eagle flew over the marketplace and shat twice in the

upturned face of a second lieutenant and that means we should double the infantry in the eastern sector.' What does that take after all? Any fool can read a chicken liver. Easiest thing in the world if you know what to look for. And one day the livers look bad so he packs up his duds and offers his services to the opposition. Can't get much saner than that.

That's what I should do. I've seen enough, haven't I? I know what's coming. Why not tell these Greeks – 'You want a prophet, you got one, baby'?

Trouble is no one ever believes me. There's a puzzle. Unvarying accuracy, no credibility. Go figure. No. I'm not Calchas after all. He can walk away. He can turn his back on his chicken livers and his tea leaves and his snakes devouring their own tails – whenever he wants. But how do you turn away when the vision is branded on your eyeballs? (*She is becoming louder and more agitated.*) Eyes open, eyes closed – sleeping or waking – no way to blink – the disaster, disaster, disaster – the holocaust burned into my eyes, into my brain – (*In agony.*) Oh, God! Make it stop! Take it away from me and let me, let me – *not see!*

Available in *The Murders at Argos / Cressida Among the Greeks*, published by Oberon Books Ltd. Reprinted by kind permission of the publisher.

ISBN: 1 84002 323 6 / 978 1 84002 323 7

KISS ME LIKE YOU MEAN IT
by Chris Chibnall

Kiss Me Like You Mean It was first performed at Soho Theatre and Writers' Centre in May 2001.

The play is set in Manchester on a hot midsummer's night. RUTH and Tony meet for the first time outside of a party at 3 a.m. Tony is instantly attracted to RUTH but she has a boyfriend, Neil. In this scene, she tells Tony a little bit about him. Strong language is used throughout the play.

RUTH: Neil likes pubs.

Reckons you can sort out all life's problems over a pint.

Gets it from his Dad. Get that man within sniffing distance of a barrel and some pork scratchings and it all comes pouring out. But most I've ever heard him say to Neil's mum is, 'Two sugars love.'

I wouldn't want to ever get like that. I've got loads to say.

If you stop talking…you might as well stop living. I mean, you only know you're alive 'cos other people, like, confirm it to you. By talking. Back to you. Don't you think?

So if you stop talking, people stop talking to you and then you sort of stop living. 'Cos it's the only sign people know you're there. And if people stop knowing you're there, how do *you* know you're there, I mean you'd start to think well is me being here just a figment of my imagination, do I actually exist at all, 'cos no bugger's talking to me and how do I know and who do I ask and if I do ask someone what if they don't reply – that'll really hit a nerve.

Oh yeah… and this pissed guy came over to me. I could smell him before he arrived, like a vat of Kouros. And he says, 'Do you believe in love at first sight or shall I walk past again?' And I said I hadn't really formed an opinion one way or the other but if he tried anything on I'd have his eye on the end of a cocktail stick. And he said, 'Leave it out, I'm only doing this for a tenner.'

Neil was the bloke who bet him.

I could have done a lot worse. I couldn't stand being alone. Sitting in. What if no-one would have me?

Can we talk about something else?

Available in *Kiss Me Like You Mean It*, published by Oberon Books Ltd. Reprinted by kind permission of the publisher.

ISBN: 1 84002 236 1 / 978 1 84002 236 0

NAVY PIER

by John Corwin

Navy Pier was first produced by Wax Lips Theatre Company in October 1997 at Strawdog Theater, Chicago, Illinois. The production then moved to the Live Bait Theater, Chicago, Illinois in January 1998.

Martin has just moved to San Francisco and takes on the persona of his once best friend, Kurt, with whom he went to college in Chicago. Martin and Kurt were fellow aspiring writers but Kurt left Martin behind when he had a short story published in an important magazine and moved to New York to make a name for himself, taking Martin's girlfriend, Iris, with him. Martin thinks that Kurt's personality was the key to his success and tries to emulate him. He meets LIV in a bar, where she works as a waitress, and asks her out, using Kurt's name. However, he realises that this is a mistake so he doesn't show for the date. He turns up at the bar the following night and, here, LIV explains what happens next. She speaks directly to the audience.

LIV: Martin said he was very sorry but he lied to me, about who he was, and he didn't want to lie to me or to anyone else anymore about who he was, and if I gave him just half a chance, he'd never lie to me again, about anything, and I would never regret it.

Pause.

This *guy…*

Everything in me told me to just walk away, forget the whole thing. But…there was something about him…

Pause.

So I told him I would think about it. You know. And he said he understood. And after that, he would come into the bar once a day. Hand me a manila envelope. And then he would walk out the door. Without a word.

Pause.

And inside the envelope was…a story, I guess. Or a poem. Little paragraph. Whatever. Each day it was something different.

He wasn't trying to 'woo' me. He was just trying to…let me know who he was. Or who he might be.

Pause.

And on Fridays, after I had been off work for four days, he would bring in four envelopes. It got to be so that Friday was my favorite day, four envelopes, four slips of paper – My favorite one was only four words long, centered in the page. 'I love your hips.' Imagine that. Someone loving these hips.

Pause.

So anyway. It lasted four weeks. Until I finally gave in. Agreed to go out with him again. Or for the first time.

Pause.

And, as it turned out, we had a great time. Great.

Available in *Navy Pier*, published by Oberon Books Ltd. Reprinted by kind permission of the publisher.

ISBN: 1 84002 199 3 / 978 1 84002 199 8

SWITCH TRIPTYCH
by Adriano Shaplin

Switch Triptych was first performed in workshop at the Ohio Theatre, New York in July 2005. The world premiere was at the Assembly Theatre as part of the 2005 Edinburgh Fringe Festival. The London season opened at the Soho Theatre and Writers' Centre in September 2005.

Switch Triptych *is set in a switchboard exchange in New York City in 1919. JUNE is English, a foreigner in New York, and it is her first day as an operator on the switchboard. Despite this, management has just announced that the operators are about to be made redundant as the company is introducing a new automatic model of switchboard. JUNE tells the other operators that she represents the union and, in this scene, tries to motivate them into solidarity against the managers of the company.*

JUNE: I hate this city. I'll admit it. I hate all the secrets. I hate the new words for things and no one cares if you learn them. I hate going into shops and feeling like I'm an intruder. An intruder on their kingdom, the chemists! The bodega, or whatever it is. Petty local despots pimping sandwiches. And nobody has any shame. They don't care if you see them, they want you to see them. And crowded! Stumble in front of a bus stop and you've got fifteen people laughing at you like they paid admission. Or not laughing, and they paid admission. Even worse. And the general loneliness. That ain't right. Nobody sees me. I know if I died, in the street, struck down from or by whatever, I wouldn't be me! I'd be a traffic jam. My corpse wouldn't be a story about me, it'd be a story about New York. And how brutal it is. And how dangerous it is.

And how exciting it is. 'Only in New York.' My living end. 'Only in New York.' Yes.

Pause.

I know why New York hates the union. Solidarity terrifies you doesn't it? You don't trust anyone! I can see why. So, yes! I take a paycheck from the Union to undo the dirt done by these tycoons. The aforementioned tycoons. Our enemy. For the gentlewomen and ladies assembled here and across your Republic. This is my work so I can hardly be faulted my subterfuge. I'm the good hands into which you should place your best interests, best intentions, and trust.

Available in *Switch Triptych*, published by Oberon Books Ltd. Reprinted by kind permission of the publisher.

ISBN: 1 84002 621 9 / 978 1 84002 621 4

BRONTË

by Polly Teale

Brontë was first performed by Shared Experience Theatre Company at the Yvonne Arnaud Theatre, Guildford, in August 2005, and subsequently at West Yorkshire Playhouse, Leeds; Warwick Arts Centre; Project Arts Centre, Dublin; York Theatre Royal; Oxford Playhouse; Liverpool Playhouse; the Lyric Hammersmith, London; and the Lowry, Salford.

This is a fictionalised account of the three Brontë sisters (CHARLOTTE, Emily and Anne) and how they came to write some of the most powerful and passionate fiction in the English language, despite being isolated on the Yorkshire moors in the 19th Century. In this scene, CHARLOTTE is discovered reading some of Emily's writing, which Emily has kept to herself. CHARLOTTE tries to persuade her to publish alongside the work of her sisters.

CHARLOTTE: Happiest when most away.
  I can bear my soul from its home of clay…
  When I am not and none beside,
  Nor earth nor sea nor cloudless sky,
  But only spirit wandering wide
  Through infinite immensity.

EMILY enters.

You must forgive me. I have done something which I should not but I came upon them and began to read before I knew what they were. Once I had begun, I could not stop.

You may be angry with me as is your right but hear me out.

I could not stop because they stirred in my heart such feeling… I know no woman ever wrote such poetry before. There is a…strange pathos. A music…wild, melancholy, utterly different from –

I am certain that these words have uncommon power. That they must be seen, be heard. That it is a crime, a shameful waste to –

I cannot believe, I will not believe that you don't secretly long to be read. What are words if not the means God gave us to reach, to grope towards one another through the darkness in hope, in hope of being found. In hope that we might become visible, to ourselves and others. Become known.

Listen to me. I have some poems of my own and Anne also. All I ask is that you allow me to send them together to a publisher and seek his opinion. We will use men's names. No one will know, but us.

Available in *Brontë*, published by Nick Hern Books. Reprinted by kind permission of the publisher.

ISBN: 1 85459 882 1 / 978 1 85459 882 0

PART TWO: TWENTIES – MALE

CRESSIDA AMONG THE GREEKS

by David Foley

Cressida Among the Greeks was first performed at the Ohio Theatre in New York City in February 2002.

Shakespeare's story of love and betrayal amidst the chaos of war, 'Troilus and Cressida', has been updated by American playwright, David Foley. TROILUS is barely 20 years old and is in love with the older Cressida. The city of Troy, in which they live, is under siege from the Greek army, so emotions are running high; however, Cressida's uncle has persuaded her at least to meet with TROILUS. During their first meeting Cressida asks TROILUS whether he enjoys war and this is his response to her. Strong language is used throughout the play.

TROILUS: There is, yes, joy in war.

[CRESSIDA: Joy?]

TROILUS: Yes. A kind of rapture. Like madness. Set loose. You become pure action – fury – heart and pulse and muscle. As if you were all-powerful, monstrous, and freed from sense.

[CRESSIDA: I see. And then...?]

TROILUS: (*Thoughtfully.*) And then – when it's over – there's a distant feeling – like a dream fading. Suddenly you stand there drenched in blood – some of it your own – and it's as if you don't remember how it happened. The fury begins to ebb from your veins, and you're drained – bereft – but somehow – holy...

[CRESSIDA: Holy?]

TROILUS: As at a sacrifice. No joy or triumph just – awe and
dread. I never go back to the city with blood still on my
armor. With blood in my hair and on my face. It isn't right.
I go to the river. I take off my armor and wash it there,
then bathe myself. My servant brings me fresh clothes
from town. But before I put them on I pray – or not prayer
really. It's as if they come to me. The men I've killed
– whose names I don't know – whose faces I couldn't
possibly remember from the blur of dust and heat. But they
come to me and say, Now we are yours. From this day
on we live in you. You are our house, and through your
corridors will sound our widows' cries and the bawling of
our children and our sad low complaints among the dead.
That's what I mean by holy.

Available in *The Murders at Argos / Cressida Among the Greeks*,
published by Oberon Books Ltd. Reprinted by kind permission of
the publisher.

ISBN: 1 84002 323 6 / 978 1 84002 323 7

CRESSIDA AMONG THE GREEKS
by David Foley

Cressida Among the Greeks was first performed at the Ohio Theatre in New York City in February 2002.

Around 1250 BC the city of Troy was under siege from the Greek army. In this version of Shakespeare's 'Troilus and Cressida', American playwright David Foley explores love and betrayal amidst the chaos of this siege. Here, HECTOR, a member of the royal family in the city of Troy, has just returned from a battle and explains to his family how he thought he had killed the great Greek warrior Achilles. Strong language is used throughout the play.

HECTOR: It was Achilles. I know the chariot. I know the shield. I know the insignia of his father's house. It was Achilles. I knew him. And he knew me – though two armies rode between us.

But he was coy – or clever. Rode just behind the lines. Just where I could see him but couldn't – get at him. I went after him. A man tried to bar my way. I spitted him on my spear and flung him behind me. Another tried to climb aboard my chariot. I split his head open with my sword. But still he kept his distance. Riding always just behind the lines. Taunting me.

I was in a fury. I redoubled my attack – killing, crushing – I hardly knew what I was doing anymore. I only wanted to get at him.

And suddenly I did. I was there, and on the open field there was just him and me. This seemed to startle him. He lost his nerve or something. Made one turn too many or too sharp and was thrown from his chariot. I hurled myself after him – grappled him right there on the ground. His sword came up and slammed against my head, stunned me, and in just that moment, he got the better of me. He reared up over me, his spear raised for the final thrust.

But he was careless. He raised his arms too high, and I thrust up with my sword – caught him just under the chin, sliced right up through the jaw and tongue and brain. His blood rained down and blinded me and I rolled free as he toppled in the mud.

I couldn't believe it! I'd got him at last! Achilles! The pride and terror of the Greeks. It seemed too simple. I went to him. I reached to claim his helmet for my trophy. I tore it off. It was – It was –

It was not – Achilles – It was –

Patroclus.

Yes. Patroclus. He'd sent the boy – his lover – out, dressed in his own armor – Why? To tease me? Bait me? Draw me on? Why? Why?

Available in *The Murders at Argos / Cressida Among the Greeks*, published by Oberon Books Ltd. Reprinted by kind permission of the publisher.

ISBN: 1 84002 323 6 / 978 1 84002 323 7

VINCENT IN BRIXTON
by Nicholas Wright

Vincent in Brixton was first performed at the National Theatre in April 2002.

Prior to becoming an artist, VINCENT VAN GOGH left Holland at the age of 20 to work in London with an international art dealing firm. Vincent in Brixton *speculates on what might have happened during the time he rents a room in Brixton. In this scene, VINCENT confides in Sam who is of a similar age and renting a room in the same house.*

VINCENT: I've got so much energy, I think I'll burst. I sit at my desk, and try to fill my head with noble thoughts. Then I see some detail in a nude by Ingres and…

He gestures in despair.

Perhaps if I found some physical outlet such as you have. That might help. There's a man who breaks the ice in the park for his morning swim. I've seen him often. But the children laugh and point at him. I wouldn't like that. No, the only thing that would stop me thinking about girls all day is a girl.

I see them every place I go. There were days last summer when there seemed to be nobody else but girls. But I can't walk up to a girl I've never met and start up a conversation.

Because I wasn't brought up like that. When I left home, my father gave me three pieces of advice. Write to your mother. Don't take up smoking. Never talk to strange girls.

…there is in fact a girl who works in the dispatch
department. Miss Beddoes. Big shoulders, broad strong
face, you'd almost think she was a Dutch girl. She's, how
can I say, she's oh, she's…

Gestures.

…well, to cut a long story short, I thought I'd ask her
to the show at the Empire. I walked to the dispatch
department thinking, this is absurd, I don't like music-
halls, I go to galleries and museums, she knows that. She'll
know that what I'm wanting to say is, 'Miss Beddoes,
I want to unbutton your blouse.' Or something worse. I
opened her door, and what did I ask her? 'Miss Beddoes,
why were you five minutes late for work this morning?' So
that was a fine success. I went back to my desk and wanted
to stick my paper-knife into me, that is how bad I felt.

Available in *Vincent in Brixton*, published by Nick Hern Books.
Reprinted by kind permission of the publisher.

ISBN 1 85459 665 9 / 978 1 85459 665 9

CAR

by Chris O'Connell

Car was first performed by Theatre Absolute, in co-production with the Belgrade Theatre, on 22 June 1999, in Coventry's Transport Museum. The play transferred to the Pleasance Theatre for the 1999 Edinburgh Festival and won the Scotsman Fringe First Award for outstanding new work. After transferring to the Pleasance Theatre, London, *Car* was awarded a Time Out Live Award – Best New Play on the London Fringe, 1999.

The play opens with the violent theft of a car by four boys. One of the boys, JASON, is in his early twenties, and, despite injuring the owner of the car, is exhilarated by the crime. JASON owes money to his drug dealers, and, fuelled by an adrenaline rush from the car theft, murders someone at their request. Here, he speaks to two of the other boys, Tim and Mark, about how his actions have changed his life forever. Strong language is used throughout the play.

JASON: The car? the car, the car, the car, the car, the car, the car, the car, the car, the car, the car, I noticed…it's red. My old man, he drives a red car. He's always driven red cars. In Japan, so he tells me, they drive white cars. Drive red cars and you're not trustworthy. My dad travels abroad and he always comes back with presents for me and my sister and he kisses my mum like he's missed her, like he's really missed her, and then he kisses me and my sister, he gets tears in his eyes and they glisten, you know when mercury breaks out of a thermometer, like it's had too much telling to do and it sends its drops, one, two, three, four, solid drops down to the floor. My dad's tears; like a mercury drop. And we're all happy to be together. We're a family on a beach, holding hands and sharing jokes. My dad tells a joke and I look up at him, I like the way his face spreads when he smiles. In my head, I'm on the beach a million times a day and the happiness gets infectious. I'm desperate for it. Beach life; give me that happy life on the beach. But then in the Crown tonight, pulling the trigger, the beach falls in and my whole life pours into the egg timer hole left gaping in the crust of the earth. Everything's changed, forever.

JASON sinks to the floor.

Available in *Street Trilogy* by Chris O'Connell, published by Oberon Books Ltd. Reprinted by kind permission of the publisher.

ISBN: 1 84002 389 9 / 978 1 84002 389 3

KID

by Chris O'Connell

Kid was produced by Theatre Absolute, in co-production with the Belgrade Theatre, Coventry. It previewed on 15 July 2003, at the Belgrade Theatre Within a Theatre. The play subsequently transferred to the Edinburgh Fringe Festival, premiering at the Pleasance Cavern.

K has had a difficult life, in and out of prison for petty crimes. After beating a boy to death he flees the country and ends up backpacking in Central America. A year later he returns to his friend Lee, and Lee's pregnant girlfriend Zoe, who both witnessed the murder. Zoe doesn't want K back in their lives as she prepares for the birth of her child: being pregnant has changed everything for her. Here, K explains to Zoe why he returned from Guatemala. Strong language is used throughout the play.

K: Tell me to go, and I'll leave.

Silence.

I was on a bus, about three months back… It was driving the coast road. I was delivering a parcel, doing odd jobs for people. I saw this girl, she turned round to look at me, she's in a seat further up the bus. She's like a backpacker. She looked like you.

Beat.

And I'm suddenly… It's like I'm waking. I feel sick, and she keeps looking at me. My head starts aching. We stop at this roadside shack and I ask for water. I'm asking people for water, and they're looking at me. I'm white, sweating.

I can see what they see: me, tiny, broken by a blast of something, the blast of remembering you, Lee, home.

Zoe sneers at him, goes to the flower bed. Plants some flowers.

That's when the headache comes, cos if I've thought of you, then you'll think of me, get inside my head, and then you'll see where I am, where I'm living. And then everyone else'll know. I can't stop my head aching, for days, weeks. I can't settle again. I want words I can understand, a conversation I can join in with. I left where I was living, found myself back in the city. (*Pause.*) I didn't know what to think.

Available in *Street Trilogy* by Chris O'Connell, published by Oberon Books Ltd. Reprinted by kind permission of the publisher.

ISBN: 1 84002 389 9 / 978 1 84002 389 3

KINGS OF THE ROAD

by Brian McAvera

Kings of the Road was first performed at the Old Museum Arts Centre in May 2002. Produced by Directions Out Production Company for Littoral Arts, as part of the Routes Festival, in association with Cathedral Arts Festival.

TJ is unconscious in a hospital bed after the bus on which he worked was blown up during the Troubles in Northern Ireland. His son, RINTY, is at his side and he recalls the stories of three generations of bus workers in their family, helped by the ghost of his grandfather. In this scene, RINTY replays the moment when he had turned 20 and explained to his father why he wanted to work on the buses. Strong language is used throughout the play.

RINTY: Da.

You know why I want to go on the buses, don'tcha?
The real reason?

Something Grandad said.
An' then you told me it later.
Frankie Carson Da.
On his retirement.
Remember you told me.
Frankie saying there was this wee girl, used to get on his bus when he first started.
And he watched her, Madeleine was her name, grow up.
Watched her courtin' with her husband-to-be.
Watched her kids grow up, her on the bus with her pram.
An' every time he seen her out walking with the pram, and he in the bus, he'd beep the horn an' wave at her, and she'd always wave back.

An' when Frankie retired, she went all over the town,
looking fer him, found his depot, and got his address.
An' she knocked on his door and she said:
'Frankie Carson, I'm the one's been looking fer you.
I grew up with you, on the buses, and this is fer you.'
An' she handed him this lovely card and inside, there were
two ten pound vouchers for Marks and Spencers.
An' she saw him looking at them, and she said, 'I'm sorry
I can't afford any more Mister Carson, but if I win the
Freestate lottery, I know where you live!'
(*A beat.*) I want a job like that Da.
Where people remember you like that... Da...
Just like Grandad... Just like you...

Available in *Kings of the Road*, published by Oberon Books Ltd.
Reprinted by kind permission of the publisher.

ISBN: 1 84002 390 2 / 978 1 84002 390 9

KISS ME LIKE YOU MEAN IT

by Chris Chibnall

Kiss Me Like You Mean It was first performed at Soho Theatre and Writers' Centre in May 2001.

TONY meets Ruth for the first time outside of a party in Manchester at 3 am on a hot midsummer's night and is instantly attracted to her. Meanwhile, Don and Edie, who are in their seventies and live on the floor above, are having a party of their own. TONY and Ruth are drawn into their world and Don advises TONY to 'grab life by the collar'. Here, TONY takes a deep breath and tells Ruth exactly how he feels. Strong language is used throughout the play.

TONY: Listen… I need to… Um… Say… I mean… I know
    we only met earlier… And I nearly set you on fire… And
    we're both going out with people. Obviously that's quite
    tricky. But… Well… You are the most beautiful woman
    I have ever laid eyes on in my entire life. I saw you and
    my heart leapt. You make me want to change my life.
    To…participate. I know it's not possible and that you have
    a boyfriend and we're not…compatible or whatever but…
    I just… I know it's stupid…but maybe just hear me out for
    a second and then you can tell me I'm an idiot and we'll
    both go back in and pretend this never happened but… I
    want to travel the world with you. I want to bring the ice
    cold Amstel to your Greek shore. And sit in silence and
    sip with you. I want to go to Tesco's with you of a Sunday.
    Watch you sleep, scrub your back, rub your shoulders,
    suck your toes. I want to write crap poetry about you, lay
    my coat over puddles for you, always have a handkerchief
    available for you. I want to get drunk and bore my friends
    about you, I want them to phone up and moan about how

little they see me because I'm spending so much time with you. I want to feel the tingle of our lips meeting, the lock of our eyes joining, the fizz of our fingertips touching. I want to touch your fat tummy and tell you you look gorgeous in maternity dresses, I want to stand next to you wide-eyed and hold my nose as we open that first used nappy, I want to watch you grow old and love you more and more each day. I want to fall in love with you. I think I could. And I think it would be good. And I want you to say yes. You might feel the same.

Beat.

Could you? Maybe?

Available in *Kiss Me Like You Mean It*, published by Oberon Books Ltd. Reprinted by kind permission of the publisher.

ISBN: 1 84002 236 1 / 978 1 84002 236 0

NAVY PIER

by John Corwin

Navy Pier was first produced by Wax Lips Theatre Company in October 1997 at Strawdog Theater, Chicago, Illinois. The production then moved to the Live Bait Theater, Chicago, Illinois in January 1998.

MARTIN and Kurt are old college friends and fellow aspiring writers. However, Kurt soon leaves MARTIN behind when he has a short story published in an important magazine and moves to New York to make a name for himself, taking MARTIN's girlfriend, Iris, with him. Here, MARTIN explains the nature of their original friendship to the audience.

MARTIN: He taught me everything I knew. Everything I know now. Kurt Mitchell. It's just that simple.

Pause.

We were in college together. Two English majors.

And what we would do is walk all over campus. That's how we'd pass the time. Walking all over Chicago; all damn day – By the end of the year, there was actually definition in my leg muscles. You could see *calves*.

Pause.

We'd talk about whatever, you know. Whatever mattered then. Whatever was affecting our lives in the present.

And it always seemed to be him. Kurt. Giving me advice. Listening to my thoughts, my doubts. Telling me how to proceed. Because I was so clueless. Really. I was. Without a clue.

Pause.

I often thought, Here is a man in control. Because he
always seemed so sure of himself. At parties. Attracting
women at will. In class, speaking articulately about
his work and that of others. He was so…adaptable. To
whatever situation. He was comfortable. At ease. Yes.

Pause.

He put me to shame.

Pause.

But I was never jealous of him. Not at all. But I must say
that I did…observe him. See why he was so successful in
all those situations. What about him, his fabric, made him
so at ease, gave him that air of confidence. I tried to learn
from him. See what I could glean from him.

Pause.

Of course I could never approach his status. Not a chance
in hell. How could I? I mean: he is he and I am me, and
there is only one of him and there is only one of me. You
see? But…I tried. I really tried.

And then, of course, after the walks, we'd go play…*air
hockey*.

There were pinball and video games, of course. But
we had no use for them. No. It was air hockey for us.
We'd play for hours. At first, it was quite friendly. But…
eventually we had to keep track of who was winning more
games. And that sure made things interesting. The friendly
insults, the bragging, they were gone as we stood there,
facing off against one another. Not saying a word. Letting

the game itself say everything. Sure, he held an edge at first. But…I'd like to think that I got better as the years progressed. I think we were about even by the time we graduated. Yes. I was at least as good as him. I think we were equals. I really do.

And then, after we were done with the air hockey, we'd go to the coffeeshop just across the street. That's where we'd finish our day. Had our own table. Sit there, drink coffee. Show each other what we'd written. We were writing like madmen then. So much *energy*. It was our own little workshop. An open and honest exchange. I showed him everything I wrote. Without hesitation. Even as I kept everything from Iris. Because I trusted him completely.

Pause.

Now: I know you should never trust anyone more than you trust yourself, but…I was so in awe of him. Wanted so much to be viewed as his equal, his peer…

Pause.

And I listened to him. Everything he told me.

Available in *Navy Pier*, published by Oberon Books Ltd. Reprinted by kind permission of the publisher.

ISBN: 1 84002 199 3 / 978 1 84002 199 8

PART THREE: THIRTIES – FEMALE

INGLORIOUS TECHNICOLOUR

by Christopher William Hill

Inglorious Technicolour was first performed at the Stephen Joseph Theatre, Scarborough, in June 2006.

Ryan Nesbitt, a 16-year-old student at a failing comprehensive in Stockton-On-Tees, is catapulted into the art scene after his art teacher shows some of his graffiti to ANTONIA FISHER, a gallery owner in London. She exhibits a set of the school's toilet doors with his graffiti in the hope of attracting buyers. Unfortunately Ryan re-paints one of the doors black before they're sold. In this scene, she receives a phone call from a dealer with a possible bidder and tries to explain the situation. Unbelievably the dealer thinks the bidder will offer £120,000. Strong language is used throughout the play.

ANTONIA: I'll go and make some coffee.

She is about to exit when her mobile rings. She hesitates, then picks up the phone.

Antonia Fisher… Hi, Fran…

Beat.

Look…we've had a bit of a disaster…

Howard paces, anxiously.

I don't know how this is going to affect the sale… I'll be honest… 'Inglorious Technicolour' is twenty-five per cent less glorious…

Howard moans.

…call it a fit of artistic pique…he's painted over it… No, *entirely*…black…

She stares at the black door, and attempts an optimistic approach.

I mean…there's a sort of nihilistic *charm* to it…

Howard stares hopefully at ANTONIA. Her optimism evaporates.

No… Sure… No, no the other three…they're exactly as you saw them… Okay… Fine… Look, I know 'sorry' doesn't really… Right… Really? How much?

Her face drops.

Oh…God…

Yes, sure… Right… Yes. Call me at home or… Yes, I'll have the mobile… If there's anything I… Yes… Okay… Sure… Look, Fran…

Fran has hung up.

…bye.

She's spoken to the Burgraaf Museum in Amsterdam. They specialise in Pop Art…

Apparently one of their buyers came to the launch. He liked the doors. Fran thinks they'll go to a hundred and twenty.

Available in *Inglorious Technicolour and Other Plays* by Christopher William Hill, published by Oberon Books Ltd. Reprinted by kind permission of the publisher.

ISBN: 1 84002 632 4 / 978 1 84002 632 0

SLEEPING DOGS

by Philip Osment

Sleeping Dogs was first performed in September 1993 by Red Ladder Theatre Company.

Sleeping Dogs *explores the tensions between Christians and Muslims during the war in the former Yugoslavia. Trouble has reached a small town in the south of the country, where Christians and Muslims have peacefully co-existed for some time. The children of the town are sent away to safety but their bus is stopped by Christian militiamen and the Muslim children are murdered. SABINA, a Muslim woman in her thirties, sent her daughter on that bus. Here, she holds her dead child and speaks to her female neighbours: Irma, Nadija and Hamida.*

SABINA: Still warm,
  She's still warm.
  While I was measuring out the flour
  She was sitting chatting to her friend.
  While I was weighing out the butter,
  Armed men stepped in front of the bus.
  While I was mixing them together,
  They shot the driver and got on board.
  While I was adding sugar
  They separated my daughter from her friend
  Lined her up with the other Muslims on the bridge.
  While I was cracking eggs
  Someone held a knife to her neck.
  While I was stirring them in,
  He slit her throat.
  As I poured the mixture into the tin
  She died.
  Feel her,

She's still warm.

She drops the knife onto the ground.

They go to comfort her.

Leave me.

Available in *Plays for Young People* by Philip Osment, published by Oberon Books Ltd. Reprinted by kind permission of the publisher

ISBN: 1 84002 272 8 / 978 1 84002 272 8

THE DARKER FACE OF THE EARTH
by Rita Dove

The Darker Face of the Earth, by the former US Poet Laureate, was first performed at the Oregon Shakespeare Festival in Ashland, Oregon, USA in July 1996 and in the United Kingdom at the Royal National Theatre in August 1999.

The Darker Face of the Earth *is an updated version of the Oedipus story but set on a plantation in South Carolina in the 1840s. PHEBE was born a slave on the plantation and is in her early teens when the play opens. However, 20 years pass and she finds herself caught up with the revolutionary ideas of a charismatic new slave, Augustus Newcastle. Here, she explains her mother's death to him.*

PHEBE: Mama worked in the kitchen until
    I was about five; that's when
    fever broke out in the quarters.
    She used to set table scraps out
    for the field hands, and I
    stuck wildflowers in the baskets
    to pretty 'em up. Mama said
    you never know what a flower can mean
    to somebody in misery.
    That fever tore through the cabins like wildfire.
    Massa Jennings said the field hands
    spread contamination and forbid them
    to come up to the house, but
    Mama couldn't stand watching them
    just wasting away – so she started
    sneaking food to the quarters at night.

Then the fever caught her, too.
She couldn't hide it long.
And Massa Jennings found out.

Gulps a deep breath for strength, reliving the scene.

Mama started wailing right there at the stove.
Hadn't she been a good servant?
Who stayed up three nights straight
to keep Massa's baby girl among the living
when her own mother done left this world?
Who did he call when the fire
needed lighting? Who mended the pinafores
Miss Amalia was forever snagging on bushes?

Mama dropped to her knees
and stretched out her arms along the floor.
She didn't have nowheres to go;
she'd always been at the Big House.
"Where am I gonna lay
my poor sick head?" she asked.

He stood there, staring
like she was a rut in the road,
and he was trying to figure out
how to get round it.
Then he straightened his waistcoat
and said: "You have put me and my child
in the path of mortal danger,
and you dare ask me what to do
with your nappy black head?"
He didn't even look at her –
just spoke off into the air
like she was already a ghost.

Woodenly.

She died soon after.

Available in *The Darker Face of the Earth*, published by Oberon Books Ltd. Reprinted by kind permission of the publisher.

ISBN: 1 84002 129 2 / 978 1 84002 129 5

PART THREE: THIRTIES – MALE

CAR

by Chris O'Connell

Car was first performed by Theatre Absolute, in co-production with the Belgrade Theatre, on 22 June 1999, in Coventry's Transport Museum. The play transferred to the Pleasance Theatre for the 1999 Edinburgh Festival and won the Scotsman Fringe First Award for outstanding new work. After transferring to the Pleasance Theatre, London, *Car* was awarded a Time Out Live Award – Best New Play on the London Fringe, 1999.

GARY's car was stolen by a gang of four boys: he tried to stop them but was injured and left for dead. Rob is the probationary officer of one of the car thieves and wants to bring GARY and the boy together, as part of a mediation process, to see if they can help each other. Rob hopes that the boy will be able to see the effect of his crime on another human being. Here, GARY describes to the audience how he feels after being contacted by Rob. Strong language is used throughout the play.

GARY: I'm in the bath and the phone rings I can hear the
phone ringing and Melanie's out for the night and I know
the answer machine's not on so I'm out of the bath and I'm
dripping across the landing to the bedroom where I answer
the phone and Robert says he hopes he didn't disturb
me and I laugh and say of course he didn't and inside I
know what he's about to ask me how he's following up
this mediation thing he mentioned before it's been in his
head and it's been in mine every minute every day and it's
going to be his question like I knew it would be and inside
I know if I say yes I'll do it it's just so I can get to see the
little bastard for the first time the one who nearly killed me
but just as I swap hands and put the receiver in my other
hand I'm feeling weak like my legs are going to give way

because I suddenly think will this mediation stuff make
me feel better or worse when I get to set eyes on him and
its going round and round my head again how it's not fair
how this has happened to me and I'm getting this sort of
phone call and this sort of pressure and how the bubble's
burst around me and the world's pouring in but I hear
myself speaking and I'm telling Robert I'll do it I'll go to
the mediation because I'm a good bloke and I want to be
a man and do what a person needs to do and I make him
understand it's not just for me it's for everyone who ever
got anything nicked and I tell Melanie when she gets in
and I've still got the wet towel round me and she says I'll
feel better for it... (*He stops.*) So. I'm trying not to think
about it... (*Beat.*) I've been trying not to think about it.

Available in *Street Trilogy* by Chris O'Connell, published by
Oberon Books Ltd. Reprinted by kind permission of the publisher.

ISBN: 1 84002 389 9 / 978 1 84002 389 3

GLADIATOR GAMES
by Tanika Gupta

Gladiator Games was first performed at the Crucible Studio in October 2005 and transferred to the Theatre Royal Stratford East in November 2005.

On the night of his release from Feltham Young Offenders Institution, Zahid Mubarek, a young British Asian, was murdered by his racist cellmate. Zahid had been sentenced to 90 days imprisonment for the theft of six pounds' worth of razor blades and interfering with a car but his killer had a prison career spanning nine years and a history of racist violence. Gladiator Games *traces the Mubarek family's pursuit of the truth. IMTIAZ AMIN is Zahid's uncle and only ten years older than him. The following monologue was reproduced from an original interview with IMTIAZ. He speaks directly to the audience. Strong language is used throughout the play.*

IMTIAZ: Apparently from the court (*Hesitates.*) ...Tanzeel told me that when he was there – it was quite poignant looking back on it now – in hindsight because it was like when the Judge said 'take him down' or whatever, Zahid just turned round to his grandad and Tanzeel and said in Punjabi, *'Me jara ow'*, it was his way of saying, 'I'm going again'. He said just the expression on his face was, was, you know, er, it was like...they was never going to see him again. You know...er...

Long pause.

At the time, my nephew and my dad thought it was pretty much the way they deal with things here. And especially dad, he believes in the system. My father's point of view was look – he's going to the Young Offenders Institute

– it's not a full-blown prison. They've got to have things in place to rehabilitate er… (*He laughs sadly.*) have things in place to sort them out so that they can lead a more productive life. Had we known this much (*Measures a speck with his fingers.*) of what Feltham was about, really, you know, it would have been different. It would have been different. I was in Holloway Prison a couple of weeks ago, a visit for the prison law course I'm doing and I met a prison officer there. He said to me, 'You look remarkably familiar', and so I told him my name. He put his arm around me and said: 'Look, I'm really, really sorry about what happened. I was working at Feltham at the time and I knew Zahid. He was a smashing lad.' This was just a couple of months ago – it really hit me.

He was very much loved – despite his problems. He was very much loved.

Available in *Gladiator Games*, published by Oberon Books Ltd. Reprinted by kind permission of the publisher.

ISBN: 1 84002 624 3 / 978 1 84002 624 5

TRAGEDY: a tragedy

by Will Eno

A reading of *TRAGEDY: a tragedy* was first held at the Royal National Theatre Studio in June 2000 and the play was first performed at The Gate Theatre, London, in April 2001.

TRAGEDY: a tragedy *is a tongue-in-cheek exploration of the media's coverage of tragic events. JOHN IN THE FIELD represents the dashing, perfectly groomed reporter on the scene of a tragedy, covering events for the television audience at home. In the play, night-time has fallen. Will the sun ever rise again? JOHN IN THE FIELD reports to Frank in the Studio and speaks to the camera.*

JOHN IN THE FIELD: It's the worst world in the world here tonight, Frank. People are all over, everywhere. Or, they were. Some, hopelessly involved with the grief here at the scene. Still others, passersby to the suffering, slowly passing by, looking, feeling, hoping and believing that they might learn something from these dark times, that they might find some clue about living, hidden in the dusk of the faces of those who have seen so much so fast, and such sadness.

Something is out there, or in here, and this is what we are watching. Or being watched by. One man came by a moment ago, and then, I felt, could not go on. We did all we could to keep him and his hope up until, after a time, his sister arrived, who had seen him wandering on her television, in the background behind me, in her living room at home. When she came and saw him here, she said, "There you are." He smiled. So that was one touching moment in an evening which has been largely bereft of the nice touches normally associated with the soft nights of this season.

Another thing I should say is, just, what an incredible job the animals have been doing out here tonight. You can perhaps see in my background the dogs going back and forth. They have been barking at the dark and generally doing those things they can usually be counted on to do, and these include: licking hands, yawning, circling before lying down, and making their tags and collars jingle. This, of course, all, as the hours grow more and more late out here, and we, it seems, learn less and less. That's what we know so far. Frank?

Available in *TRAGEDY: a tragedy*, published by Oberon Books Ltd. Reprinted by kind permission of the publisher.

ISBN: 1 84002 234 5 / 978 1 84002 234 6